j EASY NF BIO Love
Katirgis, Jane.
Meet Nat Love: cowboy and
former slave

Meet
Nat Love
Cowboy and Former Slave

Enslow Publishing
101 W. 23rd Street
Suite 240
New York, NY 10011
USA

enslow.com

Jane Katirgis and Sarah Penn

Published in 2020 by Enslow Publishing, LLC
101 W. 23rd Street, Suite 240, New York, NY 10011

Library of Congress Cataloging-in-Publication Data

Names: Katirgis, Jane, author. | Penn, Sarah, author.
Title: Meet Nat Love: cowboy and former slave / Jane Katirgis and Sarah Penn.
Description: New York : Enslow Publishing, 2020 | Series: Introducing famous Americans |
    Includes bibliographical references and index. | Audience: Grades 3–5.
Identifiers: LCCN 2018060040| ISBN 9781978511408 (library bound) | ISBN
    9781978511385 (pbk.) | ISBN 9781978511392 (6 pack)
Subjects: LCSH: Love, Nat, 1854–1921—Juvenile literature. | African American cowboys—
    West (U.S.)—Biography—Juvenile literature. | Cowboys—West (U.S.)—Biography—
    Juvenile literature. | West (U.S)—Biography—Juvenile literature.
Classification: LCC F594.L892 K38 2020 | DDC 978/.02092 [B] —dc23
LC record available at https://lccn.loc.gov/2018060040

Printed in the United States of America

To Our Readers: We have done our best to make sure all website addresses in this book were active and appropriate when we went to press. However, the author and the publisher have no control over and assume no liability for the material available on those websites or on any websites they may link to. Any comments or suggestions can be sent by email to customerservice@enslow.com.

Portions of this book originally appeared in *Nat Love: African American Cowboy*.

Contents

1 Looking for Adventure

Nat Love and his family were slaves on a tobacco plantation. Nat was born in Davidson County, Tennessee, in 1854. He had a sister, Sally, and a brother, Jordan. The Civil War ended slavery in 1865. Nat's family was free, but they had no money. Nat's father died. As a young teenager, Nat became the head of the family.

After the end of slavery in America in 1865, Nat Love left Tennessee for adventure. He went to the Wild West.

For more than 200 years, African American slaves worked on American lands. They got no pay for the work. They often worked from sunrise to sunset.

The family planted crops to make money. Meanwhile, pioneers traveled west of the Mississippi River. They went to settle unclaimed land. Many went in search of gold. Nat's goal was to see the world. He imagined the West would be full of excitement and adventure. Nat would not leave his family members until they could support themselves.

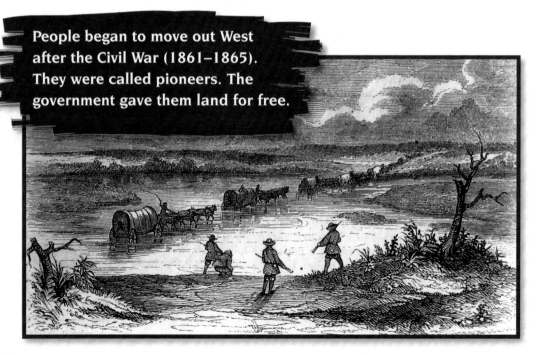

People began to move out West after the Civil War (1861–1865). They were called pioneers. The government gave them land for free.

As a teenager, Nat learned to tame wild horses. He became an excellent rider. One day he won a horse in a raffle. He sold it for $100. Nat gave half of the money to his mother. He used the rest of the money to begin his new life. On February 10, 1869, Nat headed for Dodge City, Kansas.

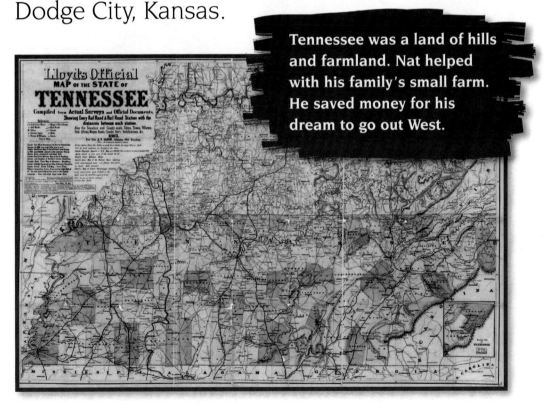

Tennessee was a land of hills and farmland. Nat helped with his family's small farm. He saved money for his dream to go out West.

Nat learned how to tame horses alone. This drawing shows cowboys breaking a wild horse.

Let's Learn More

To "break" a horse means to tame a wild horse. Taming a wild horse is hard and dangerous work. A horse trusts the cowboy who breaks it. This process makes it easy for them to work together.

2 Becoming a Cowboy

Dodge City, Kansas, was known for being a wild place. Nat Love was fifteen years old when he arrived in the town. People went to the saloons and gambled. Many cowboys would spend time there between cattle drives. Nat's excellent horseback-riding skills earned him a job as a cowboy. The Duval Outfit from Texas hired Nat. They taught him to use a gun and a lariat.

Dodge City was popular with cowboys for drinking and fighting. Nat had his first adventures in this city.

Cattle drives often took months to take a herd between ranches. Cowboys and cattle would have to battle bad storms with no shelter. Other problems were fights with American Indians, bandits, and buffalo stampedes. In 1872, Nat received a better job from the Pete Gallinger Company. He moved to their huge ranch in Arizona.

In search of better work, Nat Love moved to Gila River, Arizona. He might have lived in a house like this one made of adobe (mud brick).

Let's Learn More

In the Duval Outfit, Nat was known as Red River Dick.

A dozen cowboys or more worked a cattle drive. The drives often stretched more than a mile. Nat learned to live in the open air on cattle drives.

ON THE TRAIL.

On one cattle drive, Love traveled from Texas to Deadwood, South Dakota. The cowboys delivered almost 3,000 steer there on July 3, 1876. Over the next few days, Love entered a cowboy contest. Each cowboy had to rope, throw, tie, bridle, saddle, and mount a wild mustang horse. Love did it in the least time: nine minutes. He won $200.

Let's Learn More

Ranches raised cattle or other livestock. They would sell livestock to other ranches. Cattle drives were the earliest way of moving cattle from one ranch to another.

The top photo shows a scene from the Buffalo Bill Wild West Show. It played in towns to show people how cowboys worked. Nat ran cattle drives up to ranches in South Dakota (map).

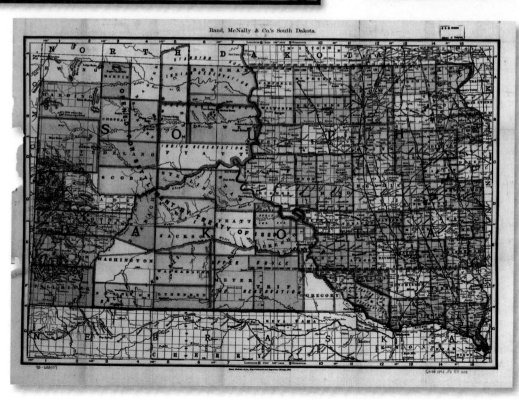

Rand, McNally & Co.'s South Dakota.

A shooting contest was held next. Love had learned to shoot a gun well. He entered the contest to try to win more money. Targets were lined up a short distance away. Whoever placed the most shots in the center of the target would win. Love placed fourteen shots in the bull's-eye. This earned him the title "Deadwood Dick."

People in the eastern United States heard about cowboys. The cowboy became a kind of hero. Artists began to show cowboys in their art.

People in the Old West used guns as common tools. A good shot could put most bullets in a black bull's-eye target. Nat was very good with his gun.

❸ Brave and Strong

One day in late 1876, Nat Love was on his own. He was looking for lost cattle in the prairie when a group of Indians attacked him. They shot him and his horse. When Love awoke, he found himself in an Indian camp. They decided to make him a member of their tribe. The Indians thought they could use a brave, strong man on their side.

Plains Indians lived in small camps. They traveled around often. They followed the buffalo herds for food.

It was uncommon for Indians to see black men. They thought black men might be white men with painted disguises. This scene shows Indians trying to rub off the "paint" of a captured black cowboy.

The Indians healed Love's wounds. He went along with this for a while. Love knew that once the tribe trusted him, he could escape. One night he stayed awake while the Indians were asleep. He quietly stole one of their best horses and escaped. Love returned to the Gallinger Company in Arizona.

Nat Love rode without a saddle when he escaped his Indian captors. He could ride any kind of horse.

My Escape—I Ride a Hundred Miles in Twelve Hours Without a Saddle

Western cities in the late 1800s were a melting pot. People of all ethnic backgrounds lived around each other.

The cowboys were surprised and happy to see Nat Love again. They had given him up for dead. Love began working again. The cowboys were known to get a bit wild. One night, they were in Fort Dodge. Love and the other cowboys were having a good time. Love decided to rope a cannon and bring it back to camp.

Nat Love drew a picture of the time he tried to steal a town's cannon. Cowboys liked to play pranks. Nat roped the cannon's barrel like he would rope a calf.

I Rope One of Uncle Sam's Cannon—Fort Dodge, Kan.

Horses are strong animals, as shown in this hand-colored engraving of an illustration by artist Frederic Remington.

Let's Learn More

Cowboys used their horses for most of their work. A horse was helpful in bringing a cow back to the rest of the herd.

Love's idea was to use it to fight the Indians. He roped the cannon and used a horse to pull on it. He quickly found out the cannon was too heavy to pull. Love was arrested. The sheriff, Bat Masterson, knew these cowboys were not bad guys. He released Nat Love.

Bat Masterson knew that most cowboys were good guys. He often overlooked their pranks.

Retired Cowboy Life

4

Nat Love fell in love when he moved to Denver, Colorado. He met a woman named Alice. Nat and Alice got married on August 22, 1889. By 1890, towns and factories began to take over the West. Trains began to move cattle across the country. This was faster, safer, and cheaper than cattle drives. Love retired from life as a cowboy.

In 1889, Denver, Colorado, was a busy city. It was once a huge cattle town. By 1890, factories drew people from the farms to work in the city.

Nat's family depended on him. By 1890, he had to think more about his family. He left the open range and got a city job.

Love needed a job to support himself and his family. He became a Pullman porter on the Denver and Rio Grande Railroad. Before he died, Love wrote a book about his adventures.

The Life and Adventures of Nat Love was published in 1907. Some people consider many cowboy stories to be "tall tales." He died in 1925.

Let's Learn More

Nat sometimes puffed up the story of his life to make it seem more exciting.

THE LIFE AND ADVENTURES
OF NAT LOVE
BETTER KNOWN
IN THE CATTLE COUNTRY AS

DEAD WOOD DICK

BY HIMSELF

While working as a train porter, Nat Love wrote the story of his life. He wanted to share his adventures with the public. The book helped tell one story about cowboy life in the American West.

Timeline

1854 — Nat Love is born into slavery in Davidson County, Tennessee.

1861-1865 — The Civil War is fought.

1865-1869 — Nat Love and his family are no longer slaves. They make a life of their own.

1869 — Nat goes to Dodge City, Kansas. He becomes a cowboy in the Duval Outfit. He moves to Texas, where their ranch is based.

1872 — Nat becomes a cowboy in the Pete Gallinger Company. He moves to their large ranch in southern Arizona.

1876 — Nat earns the title of "Deadwood Dick."

1877 — Nat tries to rope a cannon in Dodge City, Kansas.

1889 — Nat marries Alice.

1890 — Nat ends his career as a cowboy to become a Pullman porter for the railroads.

1907 — *The Life and Adventures of Nat Love* is published.

1925 — Nat Love dies.

Glossary

cannon (KAN-uhn) A heavy gun that fires large metal balls.

lariat (LA-ree-uht) A lasso or long rope used to catch animals.

legacy (LEG-uh-see) Something handed down from one generation to another.

pioneer (PYE-uh-NEER) One of the first people to work or settle in a new and unknown area.

plantation (plan-TAY-shun) A large farm found in warm climates where crops such as tobacco, coffee, tea, and cotton are grown.

Pullman porter (Puhl-man por tur) Black men who worked as porters to carry luggage on railroad sleeping cars.

slavery (SLAYV-ree) When someone is "owned" by another person and thought of as property.

stampede (stam-PEED) When people or animals make a sudden, wild rush in one direction, usually because something has frightened them.

steer (STEER) A young male of the domestic cattle family raised especially for its beef.

Learn More

Books

Baptiste, Tracey. *If You Were a Kid in the Wild West.* New York, NY: Children's Press, 2018.

Kovacs, Vic. *A Cowboy's Life.* New York, NY: PowerKids Press, 2016.

Sheinkin, Steve. *Neil Armstrong and Nat Love, Space Cowboys.* New York, NY: Roaring Book Press, 2019.

Websites

The National Museum of American History
americanhistory.si.edu

Type "Nat Love" in the search bar to find the story "Love on the Range: The Story of a Cowboy."

Nat Love
natlove.com

Presenting Nat Love's tale of courage, dedication, and great adventure.

The Wild West
thewildwest.org

Be transported into the past of the American Wild West, its history, and its legends of cowboys.

Primary Source Image List

between the Mandan people and a member of the Corps of Discovery in 1804–5.

Page 18: Photograph of an illustration by Nat Love titled *My Escape—I Ride a Hundred Miles in Twelve Hours Without a Saddle*, appearing in his autobiography, *The Life and Adventures of Nat Love*, 1907.

Page 19: Hartwell & Hamaker photograph of a scene in Phoenix, Arizona, circa 1899.

Page 20: Photograph of an illustration by Nat Love titled *I Rope One of Uncle Sam's Cannon—Fort Dodge, Kan.*, appearing in his autobiography, *The Life and Adventures of Nat Love*, 1907.

Page 21: Hand-colored woodcut of a nineteenth-century illustration by Frederic Remington.

Page 22: Photograph of William Barclay "Bat" Masterson, taken Dodge City, Kansas, between 1880 and 1885.

Page 23: Illustration of Denver, Colorado, city street, circa 1880.

Page 24: Photograph of Nat Love and his family, circa 1907, appearing in his autobiography *The Life and Adventures of Nat Love*.

Page 26: Photograph of the cover illustration by Nat Love to his autobiography *The Life and Adventures of Nat Love*; Photograph of Nat Love titled "The Close of My Railroad Career," appearing in his autobiography *The Life and Adventures of Nat Love*.

Index